THE

LIFE AND DEATH OF ABRAHAM LINCOLN.

A SERMON

PREACHED AT THE

CHURCH OF THE HOLY TRINITY,

PHILADELPHIA,

Sunday Morning, April 23, 1865,

BY THE

REV. PHILLIPS BROOKS.

PRINTED AT THE REQUEST OF MEMBERS OF THE CONGREGATION.

PHILADELPHIA:
HENRY B. ASHMEAD, BOOK AND JOB PRINTER,
Nos. 1102 AND 1104 SANSOM STREET.
1865.

"HE CHOSE DAVID ALSO HIS SERVANT AND TOOK HIM AWAY FROM THE SHEEPFOLDS; THAT HE MIGHT FEED JACOB HIS PEOPLE AND ISRAEL HIS INHERITANCE. SO HE FED THEM WITH A FAITHFUL AND TRUE HEART, AND RULED THEM PRUDENTLY WITH ALL HIS POWER."—*Psalm* lxxviii, 71, 72, 73.

HERE is a description of a great and good ruler—of the source from which God took him, of the purpose of his taking, and of the character which belonged to the rulership which he exercised.

While I speak to you to-day, the body of the President who ruled this people is lying honored and loved, in our City. It is impossible with that sacred presence in our midst for me to stand and speak of the ordinary topics which occupy the pulpit. I must speak of him to-day; and I therefore undertake to do what I had intended to do at some future time, to invite you to study with me the character of Abraham Lincoln, the impulses of his life, and the causes of his death. I know how hard it is to do it rightly, how impossible it is to do it worthily. But I shall speak with confidence because I speak to those who love him, and whose ready love will fill out the deficiencies in a picture which my words will weakly try to draw. I can only promise you to speak calmly, conscientiously, affectionately, and with what understanding of him I can command.

We take it for granted first of all, that there is an essential connection between Mr. Lincoln's character and his violent and bloody death. It is no accident, no arbitrary decree of Providence. He lived as he did, and he died as he did, because he was what he was. The more we see of events, the less we come to believe in any fate or destiny except the destiny of character. It will be our duty, then, to see what there was in the character of our great President that created the history of his life and at last produced the catastrophe of his cruel death. After the first trembling horror, the first outburst of indignant sorrow has grown calm, these are the questions which we are bound to ask and answer.

It is not necessary for me even to sketch the biography of Mr. Lincoln. He was born in Kentucky, fifty-six years ago, when Kentucky was a pioneer State. He lived, as boy and man, the hard and needy life of a backwoodsman, a farmer, a river boatman, and finally, by his own efforts at self-education, of an active, respected, influential citizen in the half-organized and manifold interests of a new and energetic community. From his boyhood up he lived in direct and vigorous contact with men and things, not as in older states and easier conditions with words and theories; and both his moral convictions and his intellectual opinions gathered from that contact a supreme degree of that character by which men knew him—that character which is the most distinctive possession of the best American nature—that almost indiscribable quality which we call in general clearness or truth, and which appears in the physical structure as health, in the moral constitution as honesty, in the mental structure as sagacity, and in the region of active life as practicalness. This one character, with many sides all shaped by the same essential force and testifying to the same inner influences, was what was powerful in him and decreed for him the life he was to live and the death he was to die. We must take no smaller view than this of what he was. Even his physical conditions are not to be forgotten in making up his character. We make too little always of the physical; certainly we make too little of it here if we lose out of sight the strength and muscular activity, the power of doing and enduring, which the backwoods-boy inherited from generations of hard-living ancestors, and appropriated for his own by a long discipline of bodily toil. He brought to the solution of the question of labor in this country, not merely a mind but a body thoroughly in sympathy with labor, full of the culture of labor, bearing witness to the dignity and excellence of work in every muscle that work had toughened and every sense that work had made clear and true. He could not have brought the mind for his task so perfectly, unless he had first brought the body whose rugged and stubborn health was always contradicting to him the false theories of labor, and always asserting the true. Who shall say that even with David the son of Jesse, there was not a physical as well as a spiritual culture in the struggle with the lion and the bear which occurred among the sheepfolds, out of which God took him to be the ruler of his people?

As to the moral and mental powers which distinguished him, all embraceable under this general description of clearness or truth, the most remarkable thing is the way in which they blend with one another, so that it is next to impossible to examine them in separation. A great many people have discussed very crudely whether Abraham Lincoln was an intellectual man or not; as if intellect were a thing always of the same sort, which you could precipitate from the other constituents of a man's nature and weigh by itself, and compare by pounds and ounces in this man with another. The fact is that in all the simplest characters the line between the mental and moral natures is always vague and indistinct. They run together, and in their best combinations you are unable to discriminate in the wisdom which is their result, how much is moral and how much is intellectual. You are unable to tell whether in the wise acts and words which issue from such a life there is more of the righteousness that comes of a clear conscience or of the sagacity that comes of a clear brain. In more complex characters and under more complex conditions, the moral and the mental lives come to be less healthily combined. They coöperate, they help each other less. They come even to stand over against each other as antagonists; till we have that vague but most melancholy notion which pervades the life of all elaborate civilization, that goodness and greatness, as we call them, are not to be looked for together, till we expect to see and so do see a feeble and narrow conscientiousness on the one hand and a bad unprincipled intelligence on the other, dividing the suffrages of men.

It is the great boon of such characters as Mr. Lincoln's, that they reunite what God has joined together and man has put asunder. In him was vindicated the greatness of real goodness and the goodness of real greatness. The twain were one flesh. Not one of all the multitudes who stood and looked up to him for direction with such a loving and implicit trust can tell you to-day whether the wise judgments that he gave came most from a strong head or a sound heart. If you ask them they are puzzled. There are men as good as he, but they do bad things. There are men as intelligent as he, but they do foolish things. In him goodness and intelligence combined and made their best result of wisdom. For perfect truth consists not merely in the right constituents of character, but in their right and intimate conjunction. This union of the mental and moral into a life of admirable simplicity is what we most admire in children, but in them it is unsettled and unpractical. But when it is preserved into a manhood, deepened into reliability and maturity, it is that glorified childlikeness, that high and reverend simplicity which shames and baffles the most accomplished astuteness, and is chosen by God to fill his purposes when he needs a ruler for his people of faithful and true heart, such as he had who was our President.

Another evident quality of such a character as this, will be its freshness or newness, so to speak. Its freshness, or readiness—call it what you will—its ability to take up new duties and do them in a new way will result of necessity from its truth and clearness. The simple natures and forces will always be the most pliant ones. Water bends and shapes itself to any channel. Air folds and adapts itself to each new figure. They are the simplest and the most infinitely active things in nature. So this nature, in very virtue of its simplicity, must be also free, always fitting itself to each new need. It will always start from the most fundamental and eternal conditions, and work in the straightest even although they be the newest ways to the present prescribed purpose. In one word it must be broad and independent and radical. So that freedom and radicalness in the character of Abraham Lincoln were not separate qualities, but the necessary results of his simplicity and childlikeness and truth.

Here then we have some conception of the man. Out of this character came the life which we admire and the death which we lament to-day. He was called in that character to that life and death. It was just the nature, as you see, which a new nation such as ours ought to produce. All the conditions of his birth, his youth, his manhood, which made him what he was, were not irregular and exceptional, but were the normal conditions of a new and simple country. His pioneer home in Indiana, was a type of the pioneer land in which he lived. If ever there was a man who was a part of the time and country he lived in this was he. The same simple respect for labor won in the school of work and incorporated into blood and muscle; the same unassuming loyalty to the simple virtues of temperance and industry and integrity; the same sagacious judgment which had learned to be quick-eyed and quick-brained in the constant presence of emergency; the same direct and clear thought about things, social, political and religious, that was in him supremely, was in the people he was sent to rule. Surely, with such a type-man for ruler, there would seem to be but a smooth and even road over which he might lead the people whose character he represented into the new region of national happiness and comfort and usefulness, for which that character had been designed.

But then we come to the beginning of all trouble. Abraham Lincoln was the type-man of the country, but not of the whole country. This character which we have been trying to describe was the character of an American under the discipline of freedom. There was another American character which had been developed under the influence of slavery. There was no one American char-

acter embracing the land. There were two characters, with impulses of irrepressible and deadly conflict. This citizen whom we have been honoring and praising represented one. The whole great scheme with which he was ultimately brought in conflict, and which has finally killed him, represented the other. Beside this nature, true and fresh and new, there was another nature false and effete and old. The one nature found itself in a new world, and set itself to discover the new ways for the new duties that were given it. The other nature, full of the false pride of blood, set itself to reproduce in a new world the institutions and the spirit of the old, to build anew the structure of a feudalism which had been corrupt in its own days, and which had been left far behind by the advancing conscience and needs of the progressing race. The one nature magnified labor, the other nature depreciated and despised it. The one honored the laborer and the other scorned him. The one was simple and direct. The other complex, full of sophistries and self-excuses. The one was free to look all that claimed to be truth in the face, and separate the error from the truth that might be in it. The other did not dare to investigate because its own established prides and systems were dearer to it than the truth itself, and so even truth went about in it doing the work of error. The one was ready to state broad principles, of the brotherhood of man, the universal fatherhood and justice of God, however imperfectly it might realize them in practice. The other denied even the principles, and so dug deep and laid below its special sins the broad foundation of a consistent acknowledged sinfulness. In a word, one nature was full of the influences of Freedom, the other nature was full of the influences of Slavery.

In general these two regions of our national life were separated by a geographical boundary. One was the spirit of the North, the other was the spirit of the South. But the Southern nature was by no means all a Southern thing. There it had an organized established form, a certain, definite, established institution about which it clustered. Here, lacking that advantage, it lived in less expressive ways and so lived more weakly. There, there was the horrible sacrament of slavery, the outward and visible sign round which the inward and spiritual temper gathered and kept itself alive. But who doubts that among us the spirit of slavery lived and throve? Its formal existence had been swept away from one state after another, partly on conscientious, partly on economical grounds, but its spirit was here, in every sympathy that Northern winds carried to the listening ear of the Southern slaveholder, and in every oppression of the weak by the strong, every proud assumption of idleness over labor which echoed the music of Southern life back to us. Here in our midst lived that worse and falser nature, side by side with the true and better nature which God meant should be the nature of Americans, and of which he was shaping out the type and champion in his chosen David of the sheepfolds.

Here then we have the two. The history of our country for many years is the history of how these two elements of American life approached collision. They wrought their separate reactions on each other. Men debate and quarrel even now about the rise of Northern abolitionism, about whether the Northern abolitionists were right or wrong, whether they did harm or good. How vain the quarrel is! It was inevitable. It was inevitable in the nature of things that two such natures living here together should be set violently against each other. It is inevitable, till man be far more unfeeling and untrue to his convictions than he has always been, that a great wrong asserting itself vehemently should arouse to no less vehement assertion the opposing right. The only wonder is that there was not more of it. The only wonder is that so few were swept away to take by an impulse they could not resist their stand of hatred to the wicked institution. The only wonder is that only one brave, reckless man came forth to cast himself, almost single-handed, with a hopeless hope, against the proud power that he hated, and trust to the influence of a soul marching on into the history of his countrymen to stir them to a vindication of the truth he loved. At any rate, whether the abolitionists were wrong or right, there grew up about their violence, as there always will about the extremism of extreme reformers, a great mass of feeling, catching their spirit and asserting it firmly though in more moderate degrees and methods. About the nucleus of Abolitionism grew up a great American Anti-slavery determination, which at last gathered strength enough to take its stand, to insist upon the checking and limiting the extension of the power of slavery, and to put the type-man whom God had been preparing for the task, before the world to do the work on which it had resolved. Then came discontent, secession, treason. The two American natures long advancing to encounter, met at last and a whole country yet trembling with the shock, bears witness how terrible the meeting was.

Thus I have tried briefly to trace out the gradual course by which God brought the character which he designed to be the controlling character of this new world into distinct collision with the hostile character which it was to destroy and absorb, and set it in the person of its type-man in the seat of highest power. The character formed under the discipline of Freedom, and the character formed under the discipline of Slavery, developed all their difference and met in hostile conflict when this war began. Notice, it was not only in what he did and was towards the slave, it was in all he did and was everywhere that we accept Mr. Lincoln's character as the true result of our free life and institutions. Nowhere else could have come forth that genuine love of the people, which in him no one could suspect of being either the cheap flattery of the demagogue or the abstract philanthropy of the philosopher, which made our President, while he lived, the centre of a great household land, and when he died so cruelly, made every humblest household thrill with a sense of personal bereavement which the death of rulers is not apt to bring. Nowhere else than out of the life of freedom could have come that personal unselfishness and generosity which made so gracious a part of this good man's character. How many soldiers feel yet the pressure of a strong hand that clasped theirs once as they lay sick and weak in the dreary hospital. How many ears will never lose the thrill of some kind word he spoke —he who could speak so kindly to promise a kindness that always matched his word. How often he surprised the land with a clemency which made even those who questioned his policy love him the more for what they called his weakness; seeing how the man in whom God had most embodied the discipline of Freedom not only could not be a slave, but could not be a tyrant. In the heartiness of his mirth and his enjoyment of simple joys; in the directness and shrewdness of perception which constituted his wit; in the untired, undiscouraged faith in human nature which he always kept; and perhaps above all in the plainness and quiet unostentatious earnestness and independence of his religious life, in his humble love and trust of God—in all, it was a character such as only Freedom knows how to make.

Now it was in this character rather than in any mere political position that the fitness of Mr. Lincoln to stand forth in the struggle of the two American natures really lay. We are told that he did not come to the Presidential chair pledged to the abolition of Slavery. When will we learn that with all true men it is not what they intend to do, but it is what the qualities of their natures bind them to do that determines their career? The President came to his power full of the blood, strong in the strength of Freedom. He came there free and hating slavery. He came there, leaving on record words like these spoken three years before and never contradicted. He had said, "A house divided against itself cannot stand. I believe this Government cannot endure, permanently, half slave and half free. I do not expect the Union to be dissolved. I do not expect the house to fall; but I expect it will cease to be divided. It will become all one thing or all the other." When the question came he knew which thing he meant that it should be. His whole nature settled that question for him. With such a man, intentions far ahead meant little. Such a man must always live as he used to say he lived, (and was blamed for saying it) "controlled by events not controlling them." And with a reverent and clear mind to be controlled by events, means to be controlled by God. For such a man there was no hesitation when God brought him up face to face with Slavery and put the sword into his hand and said, "Strike it down dead." He was a willing servant then. If ever the face of a man writing solemn words glowed with a solemn joy, it must have been the face of Abraham Lincoln, as he bent over the page where the Emancipation Proclamation of 1863 was growing into shape, and giving manhood and freedom as he wrote it to hundreds of thousands of his fellowmen. Here was a work in which his whole nature could rejoice. Here was an act that crowned the whole culture of his life. All the past, the free boyhood in the woods, the free youth upon the farm, the free manhood in the honorable citizen's employments—all his freedom gathered and completed itself in this. And as the swarthy multitudes came in ragged, and tired, and hungry, and ignorant, but free forever from anything but the memorial scars of the fetters and the whip, singing rude songs in which the new triumph of freedom struggled and heaved below the sad melody that had been shaped for bondage; as in their camps and hovels there grew up to their half-superstitious eyes the image of a great Father almost more than man to whom they owed their freedom; were they not half right? For it was not to one man, driven by stress of policy, or swept off by a whim of pity that the noble act was due. It was to the American nature, long kept by God in his own intentions till his time should come, at last emerging into sight and power, and bound up and embodied in this best and most American of all Americans, to whom we and those poor frightened slaves at last might look up together and love to call him with one voice, our Father.

Thus, we have seen something of what the character of Mr. Lincoln was, and how it issued in the life he lived.

It remains for us to see how it resulted also in the terrible death which has laid his murdered body here in our town among lamenting multitudes to-day. It is not a hard question, though it is sad to answer. We saw the two natures, the nature of Slavery and the nature of Freedom at last set against each other, come at last to open war. Both fought, fought long, fought bravely; but each, as was perfectly natural, fought with the tools and in the ways which its own character had made familiar to it. The character of Slavery was brutal, barbarous and treacherous, and so the whole history of the slave power during the war has been full of ways of warfare brutal, barbarous, and treacherous beyond anything that men bred in freedom could have been driven to by the most hateful passions. It is not to be marvelled at. It is not to be set down as the special sin of the war. It goes back beyond that. It is the sin of the system. It is the barbarism of Slavery. When Slavery went to war to save its life, what wonder if its barbarism grew barbarous a hundred-fold.

One would be attempting a task which once was almost hopeless, but which now is only needless, if he set himself to convince a Northern congregation that Slavery was a barbarian institution. It would be hardly more necessary to try to prove how its barbarism has shown itself during this war. The same spirit which was blind to the wickedness of breaking sacred ties, of separating man and wife, of beating women till they dropped down dead, of organizing licentiousness and sin into commercial systems, of forbidding knowledge and protecting itself with ignorance, of putting on its arms and riding out to steal a State at the beleaguered ballot-box away from Freedom—in one word (for its simplest definition is its worst dishonor), the spirit that gave man the ownership in man in time of peace has found out yet more terrible barbarisms for the time of war. It has hewed and burned the bodies of the dead. It has starved and mutilated its helpless prisoners. It has dealt by truth, not as men will in a time of excitement lightly and with frequent violations, but with a cool, and deliberate, and systematic contempt. It has sent its agents into Northern towns to fire peaceful hotels where hundreds of peaceful men and women slept. It has undermined the prisons where its victims starved and made all ready to blow with one blast their wretched life away. It has delighted in the lowest and basest scurrility even on the highest and most honorable lips. It has corrupted the graciousness of women and killed out the truth of men.

I do not count up the terrible catalogue because I like to, nor because I wish to stir your hearts to passion. Even now, you and I have no right to indulge in personal hatred to the men who did these things. But we are not doing right by ourselves, by the President that we have lost, or by God who had a purpose in our losing him, unless we know thoroughly that it was this same spirit which we have seen to be a tyrant in peace and a savage in war, that has crowned itself with the working of this final woe. It was conflict of the two American natures, the false and the true. It was Slavery and Freedom that met in their two representatives, the assassin and the President. And the victim of the last desperate struggle of the dying Slavery lies dead to-day in Independence Hall.

Solemnly in the sight of God, I charge this murder where it belongs, on Slavery. I dare not stand here in His sight, and before Him or you speak doubtful and double-meaning words of vague repentance, as if we had killed our President. We have sins enough, but we have not done this sin, save as by weak concessions and timid compromises we have let the spirit of Slavery grow strong and ripe for such a deed. In the barbarism of Slavery the foul act and its foul method had their birth. By all the goodness that there was in him; by all the love we had for him, (and who shall tell how great it was?) by all the sorrow that has burdened down this desolate and dreadful week, I charge his murder where it belongs, on Slavery. I bid you to remember where the charge belongs, to write it on the door-posts of your mourning houses, to teach it to your wondering children, to give it to the history of these times, that all times to come may hate and dread the sin that killed our noblest President.

If ever anything were clear, this is the clearest. Is there the man alive who thinks that Abraham Lincoln was shot just for himself; that it was that one man for whom the plot was laid? The gentlest, kindest, most indulgent man that ever ruled a State! The man who knew not how to speak a word of harshness, or how to make a foe! Was it he for whom the murderer lurked with a mere private hate? It was not he but what he stood for. It was Law and Liberty; it was Government and Freedom against which the hate gathered, and the treacherous shot was fired. And I know not how the crime of him who shoots at Law and Liberty in the crowded glare of a great theatre differs from theirs who have levelled their aim at the same great Beings from behind a thousand ambuscades and on a hundred battle-fields of this long war. Every General in the field and every false citizen in our midst at home, who has plotted and labored to destroy the lives of the soldiers of the Republic, is brother to him who did this deed. The American nature, the American truths, of which our President was the annointed and supreme embodiment, have been embodied in multitudes of heroes who marched unknown and fell unnoticed in our ranks. For them, just as for him, character decreed a life and a death. The blood of all of them I charge on one same head. Slavery armed with Treason was their murderer.

Men point out to us the absurdity and folly of this awful crime. Again and again we hear men say "It was the worst thing for themselves they could have done. They have shot a representative man, and the cause he represented grows stronger and sterner by his death. Can it be that so wise a devil was so foolish here? Must it not have been the act of one poor madman, born and nursed in his one reckless brain?" My friends, let us understand this matter. It was a foolish act. Its folly was only equalled by its wickedness. It was a foolish act; but when did sin begin to be wise? When did wickedness learn wisdom? When did the fool stop saying in his heart "There is no God," and acting godlessly in the absurdity of its impiety? The cause that Abraham Lincoln died for shall grow stronger by his death; stronger and sterner. Stronger to set its pillars deep into the structure of our nation's life; sterner to execute the justice of the Lord upon his enemies. Stronger to spread its arms and grasp our whole land into freedom; sterner to sweep the last poor ghost of slavery out of our haunted homes. But while we feel the folly of this act, let not its folly hide its wickedness. It was the wickedness of Slavery putting on a foolishness for which its wickedness and that alone is responsible, that robbed the nation of a President and the people of a father. And remember this, that the folly of the Slave power in striking the representative of Freedom, and thinking that thereby it killed Freedom itself, is only a folly that we shall echo if we dare to think that in punishing the Representatives of Slavery who did this deed, we are putting Slavery to death. Dispersing armies and hanging traitors, imperatively as justice and necessity may demand them both, are not the killing of the Spirit out of which they sprang. The traitor must die because he has committed treason. The murderer must die because he has committed murder. Slavery must die because out of it and it alone, came forth the treason of the traitor and the murder of the murderer. Do not say that it is dead. It is not, while its essential spirit lives. While one man counts another man his born inferior for the color of his skin, while both in North and South prejudices and practices, which the law cannot touch, but which God hates, keep alive in our people's hearts the spirit of the old iniquity, it is not dead. The new American nature must supplant the old. We must grow like our President in his truth, his independence, his religion, and his wide humanity. Then the character by which he died shall be in us, and by it we shall live. Then Peace shall come that knows no War, and Law that knows no Treason, and full of his spirit, a grateful land shall gather round his grave, and in the daily psalm of prosperous and righteous living, thank God forever for his Life and Death.

So let him lie here in our midst to-day, and let our people go and bend with solemn thoughtfulness and look upon his face and read the lessons of his burial. As he paused here on his journey from his western home and told us what by the help of God he meant to do, so let him pause upon his way back to his western grave and tell us with a silence more eloquent than words how bravely, how truly by the strength of God he did it. God brought him up as he brought David up from the sheepfolds to feed Jacob, his people and Israel his inheritance. He came up in earnestness and faith and he goes back in triumph. As he pauses here to-day, and from his cold lips bids us bear witness how he has met the duty that was laid on him, what can we say out of our full hearts but this—"He fed them with a faithful and true heart and ruled them prudently with all his power." The *Shepherd of the People!* that old name that the best rulers ever craved. What ruler ever won it like this dead President of ours? He fed us faithfully and truly. He fed us with counsel when we were in doubt, with inspiration when we sometimes faltered, with caution when we would be rash, with calm, clear, trustful cheerfulness through many an hour when our hearts were dark. He fed hungry souls all over the country with sympathy and consolation. He spread before the whole land feasts of great duty and devotion and patriotism on which the land grew strong. He fed us with solemn, solid truths. He taught us the sacredness of government, the wickedness of treason. He made our souls glad and vigorous with the love of Liberty that was in his. He showed us how to love truth and yet be charitable—how to hate wrong and all oppression, and yet not treasure one personal injury or insult. He fed *all* his people from the highest to the lowest, from the most privileged down to the most enslaved. Best of all, he fed us with a reverent and genuine religion. He spread before us the love and fear of God just in that shape in which we need them most, and out of his faithful service of a higher Master who of us has not taken and eaten and grown strong. "He fed them with a faithful and true heart." Yes, till the last. For at the last, behold him standing with hand reached out to feed the South with Mercy and the North with Charity, and the whole land with Peace, when the Lord who had sent him called him and his work was done.

He stood once on the battle-field of our own State, and said of the brave men who had saved it words as noble as any countryman of ours ever spoke Let us stand in the country he has saved, and which is to be his grave and monument, and say of Abraham Lincoln what he said of the soldiers who had died at Gettysburg. He stood there with their graves before him, and these are the words he said : " We cannot dedicate, we cannot consecrate, we cannot hallow this ground. The brave men who struggled here have consecrated it far beyond our power to add or detract. The world will little note nor long remember what we say here, but it can never forget what they did here. It is for us the living rather to be dedicated to the unfinished work which they who fought here have thus far so nobly advanced. It is rather for us to be here dedicated to the great task remaining before us, that from these honored dead we take increased devotion to that cause for which they gave the last full measure of devotion; that we here highly resolve that these dead shall not have died in vain; that this nation, under God shall have a new birth of freedom, and that Government of the people, by the people and for the people shall not perish from the earth."

May God make us worthy of the memory of ABRAHAM LINCOLN.

Printed in Dunstable, United Kingdom